GLOW UP LEADERSHIP WORKBOOK

Lead Yourself First,
Then Lead Everything Else

STEPHANIE WILLIAMS, MBA

Entrepreneur | Strategic Business Consultant |
Real Estate Investor and Mentor

B&B
BOOKED & BRANDED
PUBLISHING

COPYRIGHT

Published by Booked and Branded Publishing
www.bookedandbrandedpublishing.com
ISBN: 978-1-969369-23-0
First Edition 2025

Printed in the United States of America:

📩 hello@bookedandbrandedpublishing.com

TABLE OF CONTENTS

TABLE OF CONTENTS

TABLE OF CONTENTS

TABLE OF CONTENTS

WELCOME

How to Use This Workbook

This workbook is your guided space to practice, reflect, and apply the Glow Up Leadership principles. Use it daily, weekly, or during seasons when your leadership is being stretched.

It is built for action — because leaders don't just read, they implement.

CHAPTER 1

Dedication Prompt: Why Am I Here?

What kind of leader do I want to become?

Who will be impacted by my growth?

How will my leadership look one year from now if I stay consistent?

CHAPTER 2

The Leadership Mirror: Leading Yourself First

Write 3 daily habits that reflect integrity.

Current Habits

1. ____

2. ____

3. ____

Upgraded Habits

1. ______________________________

2. ______________________________

3. ______________________________

Prompt: If my team copied my habits for 90 days, what culture would they create?

CHAPTER 3

Confidence Audit: Authentic vs. Performance

Checklist: Mark ✓ where true for you.

- ☐ I prepare deeply before big moments.
- ☐ I rely on looking confident instead of being competent.
- ☐ I hide mistakes out of fear.
- ☐ I study my craft weekly.
- ☐ I compare myself often.
- ☐ I can admit when I don’t know something.

Reflection: Where am I performing instead of leading authentically?

CHAPTER 4

The Vision Map: 90-Day Leadership Sprint

Use the V.I.S.I.O.N. model: Vivid, Instructive, Sequenced, Inclusive, Observable, Narrative.

What picture of the future do I see?

What milestones matter in 30/60/90 days?

What story will I tell to get others excited?

CHAPTER 5

EQ Self-Check: Four Moves of Emotional Intelligence

Self-Awareness:
I notice when I'm triggered by...

Self-Management:
When I pause, I choose to…

Social Awareness:
In meetings, I sense unspoken…

Relationship Management:
I can repair trust by…

CHAPTER 6

Feedback Practice: The 3-Sentence Script

Reflection box: Write one real feedback conversation you need to have this week.

"What I'm seeing is..."

"The impact is…"

"The standard/support is…"

CHAPTER 7

Communication Reset: The 4C Message Builder

CLEAR	CONCISE	CONCRETE	COMPELLING

Exercise: Rewrite a recent email, meeting note, or announcement using all 4.

CHAPTER 8

Meeting Blueprint: Designing Effective Sessions

30-Minute Meeting Template

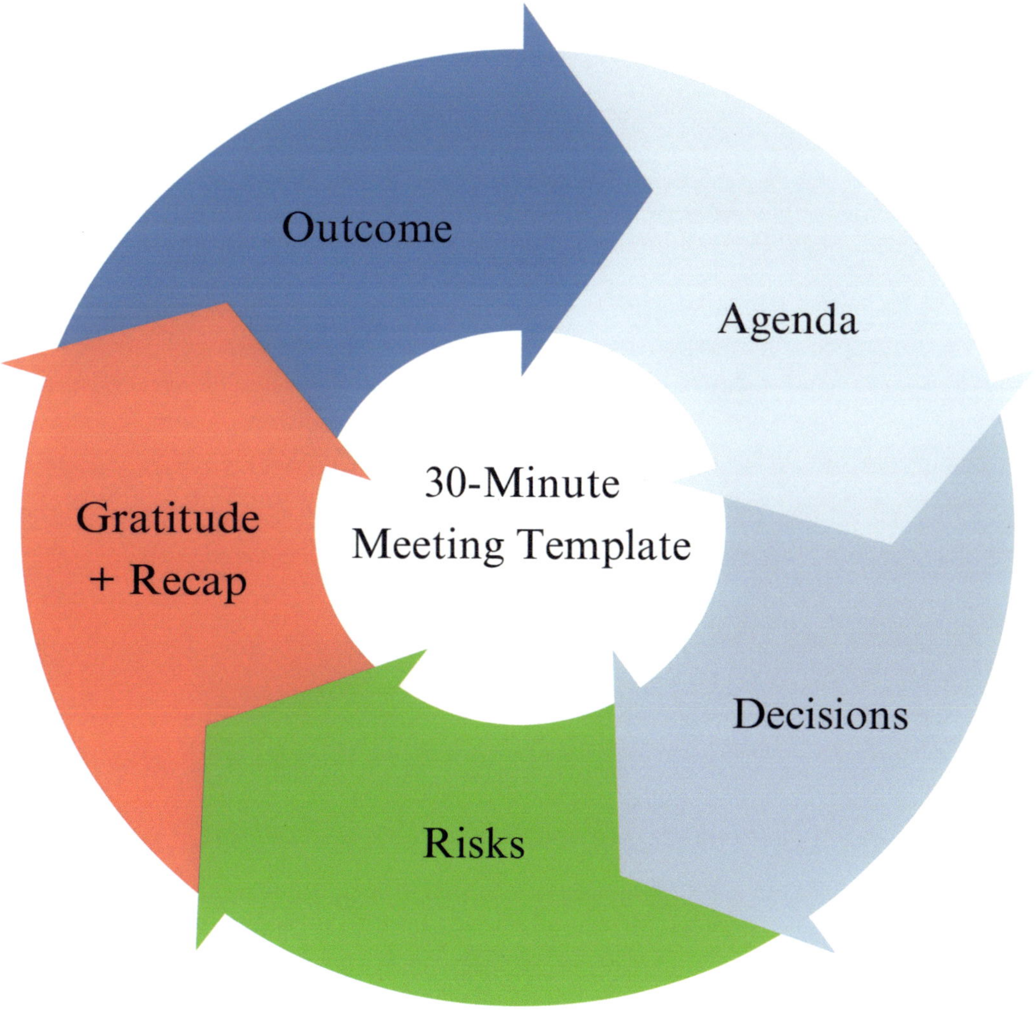

CHAPTER 9

Boundary Builder: The B.O.L.D. Script

BOUNDARY I NEED	SCRIPT I'LL USE	SUPPORT I NEED

SAMPLE SCRIPT:

"To protect delivery quality, I need 24 hours for review. If urgent, text me with 'red.' If we miss the window, it moves to Monday."

CHAPTER 10

Burnout Signals: Catching It Early

CHECKLIST:

- ☐ I'm cynical instead of curious.
- ☐ I delay decisions.
- ☐ Sleep/Joy is shrinking.
- ☐ I avoid hard conversations.

Reflection: What will I adjust this week to protect my energy?

CHAPTER 11

Decision Framework: The R.A.P.I.D. Loop

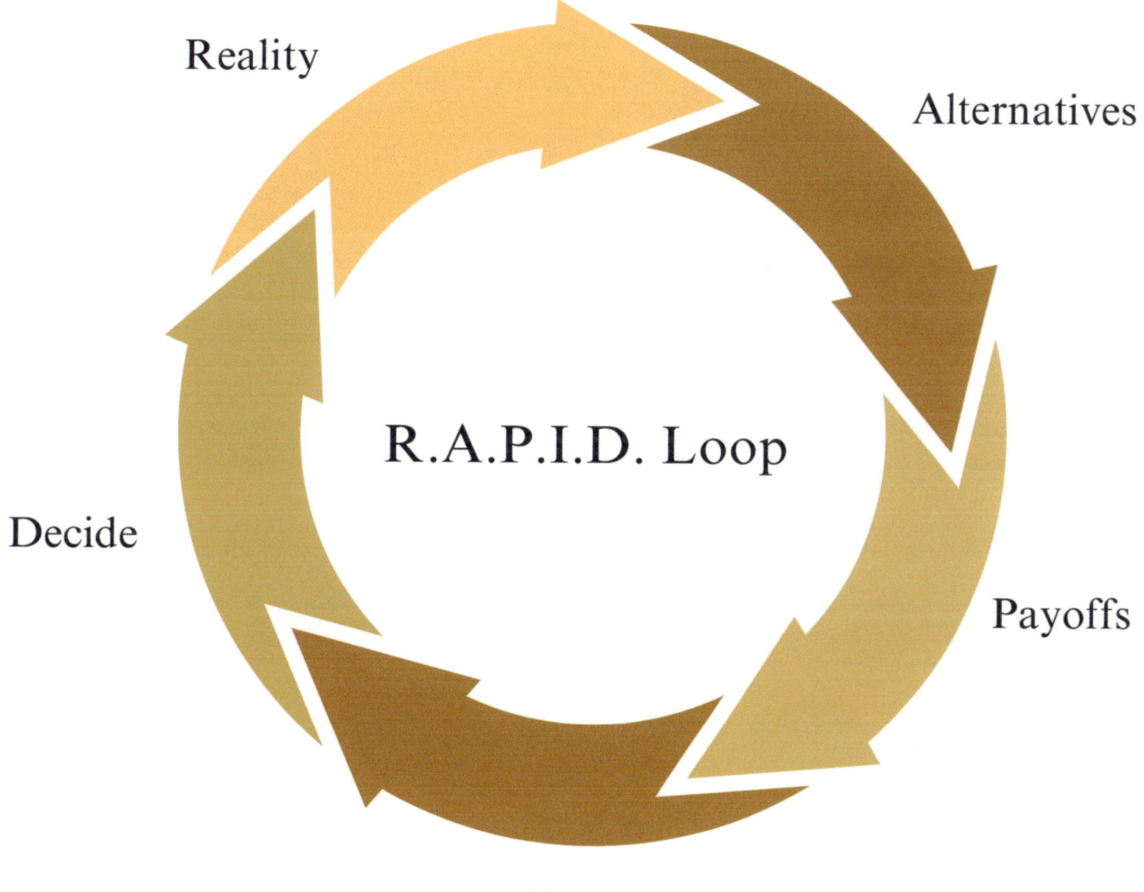

RISK STATEMENT

Risk Statement Builder: Communicating Choices

"We are choosing [option] for [X days] because [reason]. Success looks like [metrics]. If [risk], we pivot to [option]."

CONFLICT MAP

Turning Tension Into Progress

Prompt: What truth do I need to say sooner?

Issue	What's Really at Stake	Best Constructive Action

Leading Through Transition

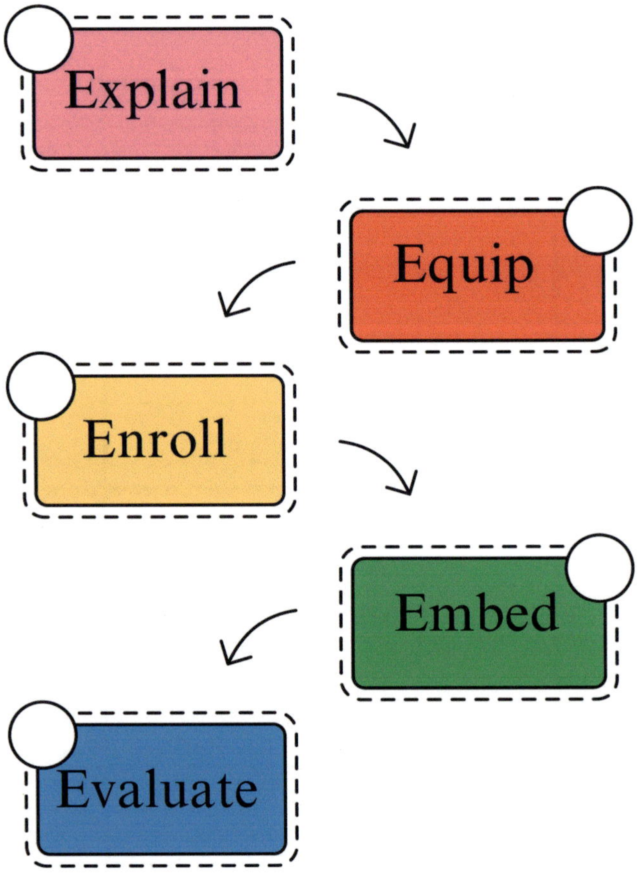

Role Clarity & Outcomes

Worksheet

Role	Top 3 Outcomes	Metrics	Check-in Rhythm

Building Other Leaders

Prompt: What can only I do? What can I teach others to own?

Task	Owner	Deadline	Guardrails	Support

LEGACY MAP

What Outlives You

Reflection: If I stepped away for 90 days, what would break? What system can I create to prevent that?

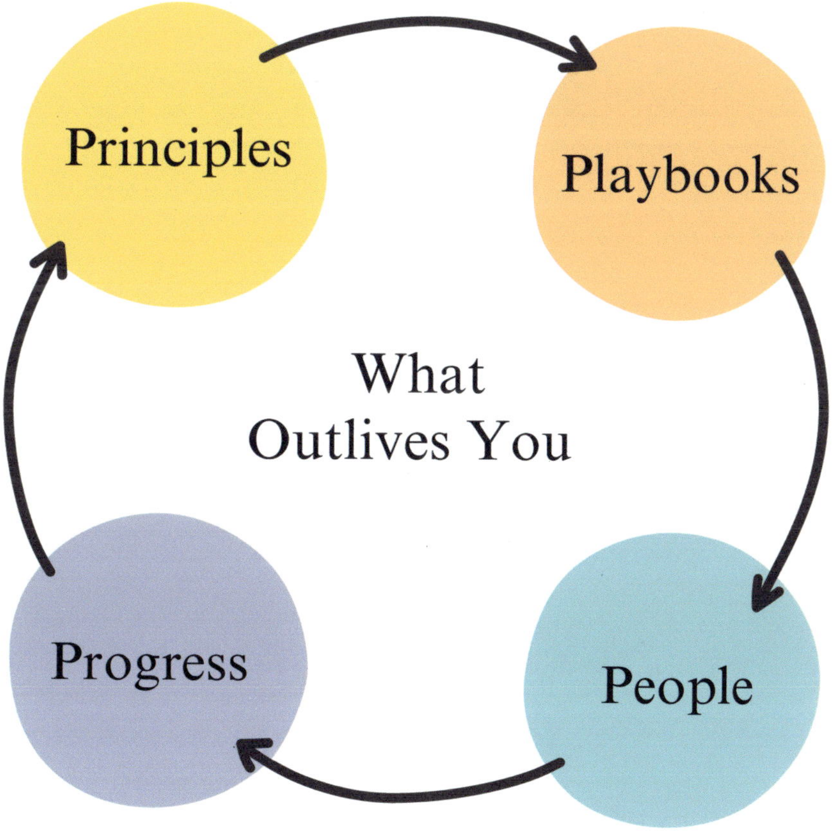

FINAL COMMITMENT

Signed Leadership Pledge

Certificate-style wording:

Glow Up Leadership Pledge:

"I commit to leading myself first so I can lead everything else with clarity, courage, and authenticity."

Signature: ______________________________

Date: ___________________________

WORK WITH ME

Your story has the power to create influence, income, and impact. If you're ready to turn your ideas into a professionally written, branded, and published book — I'd love to help.

At Booked and Branded Publishing, we specialize in:

- Ghostwriting premium books with speed and strategy
- Designing luxury-level workbooks and publishing packages
- Creating customized author branding and marketing assets

Visit

Website: www.bookedandbrandedpublishing.com

Email: hello@bookedandbrandedpublishing.com

to explore packages and book a consultation.

Let's build your legacy together.

Tagline: Where hustle meets strategy.